Dedication

This work of art is dedicated to the many names and faces who have contributed to the events that are the lines and verses of my thoughts. A special thank you to my mother, Ozell Kennedy, who has always encouraged me and given me excellent motherly guidance. To my husband, Charles Burris, who has been by my side through the lines and the verses. To my grandchildren, I would like to say always work hard to fulfil your destiny. I would also like to pay a special tribute to my dear friend, Roberta Dawson, who has been kind and patient as well as creative in helping me to do the hard work that it took to perfect this work of art.

I Finally Got It Out of My Head

© 2020 Annie G Burris

All rights reserved. This book and any parts thereof may not be reproduced in any form, stored in any retrieval system, or transmitted in any form by any means—electronic, mechanical, photocopy, recording, or otherwise—without prior written permission of the publisher, except as provided by United States of America copyright law.

Season's Greetings

Oh

Oh Christmas tree is the evergreen decorated to celebrate this day

Oh Little town of Bethlehem is where in a manger he lay

Oh holy night Joseph and Mary traveled unable to find a room at any inn

For she was to give birth to God's only begotten son sent to save us from our sin

Gifts given to this baby were not just bottles diapers rattles and things

They brought silver, gold, frankincense, and myrrh: gifts only given to Kings

Oh come all ye faithful bringing good tidings and lots of cheer

Oh come let us adore him as we share wishes of Merry Christmas and Happy New Year

While

While visions of sugarplums danced in children's heads and adults dream of a Christmas that's white

While nativity scenes both live and figurine tell the story of that great night

While carolers go door to door singing and people give gifts to show they care

Over fields and fountains hills and mountains the story is being told everywhere

So deck your halls with boughs of holly while your silver bells ring

Share memories from Christmases past while making memories for Christmases to come

And join us in the Christmas tune This Christmas while we sing

It's Not About

It's not about frosty
It's not even about Santa Claus
It's not about a toy filled sleigh
Nor reindeer paws

It's about a savior
Born in a manger
Sent to save us all from Sin
And to protect us from hurt harm and danger

When the angel visited Mary
She had absolutely no pre-conception
Of the greatness to come
Her immaculate conception

Nor could the shepherds in the field
Who saw the star that night
Ever could have fathomed
The magnitude of its light

So while Frosty The Snowman
And here comes Santa Claus are fun songs we sing
Still *Away In A Manger* and *Joy To The World*
Eco the greatness of our King

So yes sing Christmas carols
And give gifts to celebrate the season
Always keeping in mind
Jesus is the reason

Where is He?

Where is that baby boy who was born in a manger
Sent to save us from our sin
And to protect us from all hurt harm and danger

Where is that young man who preached till He was thirty-three
Then on the cross He died
He took the keys to death and hell
And the grave He denied

Well if I can convince you to believe
What I already know then you, too will find
You can make Him Lord and Savior of your life
And not just a figment of your mind

And if I can convince you to believe
He was born died and rose to set us free
Then you, too will have the answer the question
Where is He?

Funny

Toes

Toes are funny things
On them we stand and walk
I wonder what they would say
If they could only talk

Slow down my friend
You are walking at such a fast pace
I can tell by your movement
You have no time to waste

Do not stand in long lines
Standing still makes me hurt
Slow down on your running
You do not have to rush to flirt

You always wear tight socks
And they put me in a jam
You are suffocating me
Who do you think I am

You do not treat me fairly
When you get your new shoes
So others won't know how big your fee are
You by ones instead of twos

You really hurt my feelings
I just bet they would say
So think about your toes
And do not treat them this way

So think about your toes
And think about them twice
And just if they could talk
They would say something very nice

A Cold

A cold is very nasty
And makes you feel very bad
And when you have a fever
It makes you very sad

A cold seems to be deadly
For it you seem to never rid
It is about the worst thing
Even if you are not a kid

To have a cold is awful
And this for all is true
So if you have a cold
I will keep away from you

Love and Family

The Baby

He is a special kid
Such a cute little baby
When asked if I love having him
The answer is never maybe

Although he gets into things
He is still so sweet
And I open the door after school
His is the first face I meet

He is a very active kid
So we get along very well
He has a very pretty but odd name
His name is Jermelle

He is almost two now
And he is very smart
He is a precious baby
And so dear to my heart

He is a very special kid
He is so much fun
In my book of special kids
Jermelle is number one

It Takes Two

It takes two to marry
To make a family
When you say I do
It means you and the other party

It takes two for things to work
And one cannot do it all alone
For there is great sadness
When one of the parts is gone

It takes two to make it all work out
To see the other through
For any and everything
It takes two

As a family it takes two to be a great success
It is always a need for the other
Though sometimes no one will confess

For we need each other
To have a family
And to have two
Is the way it should always be

A Family

A family is a group
Loving one another
With brotherly love
Or as a father and a mother

A family gets along
Through thick and thin
Not looking at what may be wrong
But staying until the end

A family does not judge
Or cut his brethren down
No matter what the problem
Family is always around

To a family it does not matter
Whether you cannot hear, talk or see
So why is it that they use the title
'The Harding Family''

Father

F is being familiar
With everything you do

A is all the love I have
In my heart for you

T is taking time
To show me that you care

H is having enough heart
Thanks for being there

E is everything you do
In such a special way

R is right down to the point
Happy Father's Day

The Wish of a Mother

Every mother wishes
for a very healthy child
Wish that when they grow up
Their lives won't be lived wild

They wish the best for them
And help them all they can
For some day their little girl or boy
Will be a woman or a man

For they wish that as they grow old
They will grow smart
A child is very dear
To a mother's heart

They will often get you upset
But you will calm down
This just to say I love you
And it is nice to have you around

United

United we will stand
Separated we are defeated
You should treat others
As you would like to be treated

For pain is great
Among those who say they care
Because of mistreatment
And not being fair

United we can conquer
All that we must defend
United as one together
Until the very end

Being united is special
For you feel you belong
Being united should always
Bring about a happy song

Being united, a great feeling
For the land of the free
For it is the feeling of triumph
That should ring eternally

True Love

My love is very true
I love you yes indeed
You are all I want
And you are all I need

I love you truly
From the depths of my heart
To stay together forever
I wish that we may never part

My love for you is real
As real as love can be
And I believe
Your love is the same for me

For love is not a play thing
And I do not see it that way
I love you very much
And it is here to say

My love is undying
It will forever live
And with you in my life
My love I can freely give

Give you all my love
Like to no one before
And as my love grows stronger
I deeply know for sure
That our bond is sacred
It will always endure

My Love

You are my wonderful love
For you my love is true
Our love is everlasting
And it is never overdue

You are my only love
With you I wish to stay
For our love is forever
And I like things that way

Love is a challenge
It gets stronger everyday
Sometimes I keep silent
When I should have something to say

You are the one I love
That is the way it will always be
My love for you is forever
And I hope that your love is the same for me

To see you each day
Is what in my heart I so desire
For when you kiss my lips
It is set on fire

My love for you is growing
And getting stronger and stronger
To be away from you
I cannot stand it any longer

You are the one I love
You're a lover and a friend
To you I dedicate all feelings and thoughts within

And just to reassure you that this
True love is for real
When I often think of you
Love is all that I can feel

Him

There is a special person
Who is in my life
I love him very much
And will soon be his wife

He is a mature person
He is shy in his own way
Yet when I am down
He knows just what to say

His love is very strong
For it has captured me
He is never selfish
And his heart is always free

He is very mysterious
Yet so loving and kind
He is the only guy
That could ever get to my mind

He has a great family
They always seem to care
I am delighted to see them
I love going there

If he gets angry
He always walks out
And returns later, calmed down
With his situation ready to talk about

He is such a great person
I love him very much
He has many values
In love he has the touch

I love this person dearly
And my love is true
This person, Charles Alexander Burris
Is none other than you

You

There is a special person
I see most every day
When I am sick of everything
They know just what to say

When I need a friend
They are always there
They show lots of affection
They show me that they care

They always cheer me up
When I am very down
They always make me smile
When I wear a frown

This is a special person
Who in friendship is very true
This person is inspiring
And this person is you

Inspiration

I am B-L-E-S-S-E-D

I'm B-L-E-S-S-E-D
You know I am blessed because he lives in me

I was walking one afternoon through this neighborhood
I saw some homeboys and yeah they were up to no good
The devil told me homegirl you gonna be shot
But I retaliated and I said no I'm not
Because my Bible tells me no weapon formed against me shall prosper

I'm B-L-E-S-S-E-D
You know I am blessed because he lives in me
I'm B-L-E-S-S-E-D
You know I am blessed because he lives in me

I got a call from the daycare saying that my son was sick
His temperature was high and that I needed to come quick
The first thought the devil tried to put in my head
Was by time you get there homegirl he'll be dead
But I retaliated and this is what I said
My Bible tells me by his stripes we were healed

I'm B-L-E-S-S-E-D
You know I am blessed because he lives in me
I'm B-L-E-S-S-E-D
You know I am blessed because he lives in me

There was a terrible storm late one night
My daughter ran into my room filled with fright
Crying and screaming she jumped in my bed
I patted her gently and this is what I said
God is not a God of fear but of love power and a sound mind
You know I am blessed because he lives in me

I'm B-L-E-S-S-E-D
You know I am blessed because he lives in me
I'm B-L-E-S-S-E-D
You know I am blessed because he lives in me

So if you are here today and Jesus is not in your heart
When the altar call is made please do the thing that's smart
Step forward raise your hand ask Jesus to come in
Believe he died and rose again to forgive you for your sin
Then when times get hard in your life you will truly see
With Jesus living in your heart that you'll be blessed like me

I'm B-L-E-S-S-E-D
You know I am blessed because he lives in me
I'm B-L-E-S-S-E-D
You know I am blessed because he lives in me

What Makes Me Smile

When I was very little
I liked to run and play
Now that I am older
I act a different way

Now that I am older
I not only think of things
Like merry go rounds monkey bars
Sliding boards and swings

I think about the future
And what the future holds
I think about teaching
And many other goals

I think about my life
and making it worthwhile
When I think about these things
That's what makes me smile

Ignite Your Passion

As I stand before the mirror
It is not who I am that I see
I must look deeper than my reflection
To find the real me

Who I am is the things that I do
As well as the things I say
Who I am is the impact I have on others
While living my day today

Wow my reflection has
Two eyes a nose two lips and also two ears
Who I am is able to share a smile
As well as shed some tears

Who I am has a passion
And a purpose in life
It's my desire to inspire to be a good person
And a great wife

So take the opportunity to look in the mirror
And take the time to think things through
Look deeper than your reflection
To find the real you

And when you find out who you are
Then you will be able to start
Igniting your passion
And living the purpose in your heart

He Already Knew

He's the Alpha And Omega
So He already knew
The challenges we would face
And the things that we would go through

He knew you would ask for that car
He knew you would pray for that house
He even knew by the gleam in your eye
Who you would choose to be your spouse

As He walked up Calvary hill that day
He already knew
To die for our sins sickness and all our disease
Was what He was about to go do

As He hung between the two thieves
He already knew
His death burial and resurrection
Was what He was about to go through

He already knew as He talked to the Father
In that final hour
He would send us the Holy Ghost as a comforter
And endow us with power

So as you go to your knees to pray
If your shoulders feel they weigh a ton
Just remember He already knew
So it's all already done

The Bible says His promises are yes and amen
And in His word we have no doubt
So because He knew what He knew
Yet He still did what He did
Let's praise Him with a shout!

Where Is Your Smile?

I don't always wake up in the morning happy
Sometimes I even have the nerve to wear a frown
Sometimes I need to be reminded of things I take for granted
I need to be lifted up when I'm down

And if you should see me and I am not smiling,
Please tap me on my shoulder and ask where is your smile?

Sometimes I get so caught up in thought and forget that others are there
Turning my frown upside down yet unaware
And when I come down I notice people staring at me
Because a smile on my face is what they usually expect to see

So if you should see me and I am not smiling,
Please tap me on my shoulder and ask where is your smile?

It doesn't cost anything to give a smile away
Realize it not only brightens someone else's, but also your day
So don't leave your smile at home on the shelf
But remember your purpose in life is others and not yourself

So if you should see me and I'm not smiling,
Please tap me on my shoulder and ask where is your smile?

And if I should see you and you're not smiling,
I'll just tap you on your shoulder and ask where is your smile?

So if you should see me and I'm not smiling,
Please tap me on my shoulder and ask where is your smile?

My Feelings

Me

I am a different person
Unlike others I do not see well
But my life history
I have a lot to tell

I was blind from birth
And went to a special school
But I am not dumb
No I am not a fool

I have a very good mind
I try to use it a lot
Although I have poor sight
I use what I have got

I do my work differently
I don't do it in class
But I am working hard
So that I too, can pass

I do my very best to get along with people
But everyone isn't like me
Sometimes others don't realize
Through our differences, alike we can be

Vision Without Sight

It is holding on to a dream
And never letting it go

It is learning new things
The things that we do not know

It is always being ready
To do or try something new

To see is helping others
To find their way through

A Shape

You should have a shape
Neither too fat or thin
But your real shape
Is how you are shaped within

And if within your body
You are shaped well
Then with mind and intellect
You will have a story to tell

Life

Life is a bird
Singing in a tree

Life is my mother
Spelling words to me

Life is a teacher
Teaching from a book

Life is what I expect
That is my outlook

Life is important
Until my very death

So I will use wisely
The time that I have left

Am I

Am I a bad person
Say so if it is true
Have I ever done anything
that would hurt you

Am I a person who seems fun
Or do I seem to be a pain
Do I make you feel good
Or drive you insane

Take a good look at me
And see if I am so bad
If so I will do my best to change
For this makes me real sad

Am I a prompt person
Or am I always late
Am I easy to get along with
Or am I a rude classmate

Do you like me as I am
Or should I make a great change
For if that is what I need
I myself, that can arrange

I will be a better person
You just wait and see
You will be able to say I know that girl
And that girl will be me

For I will be popular
And people will say
I like her personality
And want to be that way

Anger

Anger is not the answer
It will not get you very far
When you control your anger
You show just who you are

If you control your anger
And do it very well
Others pay attention
And may learn to not let their head swell

Others are watching you
And how you handle things
Because when you show your anger
All the more anger it brings

So learn to control your anger
And learn to do it well
Keep these thoughts in mind
When your head begins to swell

And you will control that old monster
That lives deep inside
As others compliment you
You won't say that I lied

So take these words of wisdom
Although you may already know
And calm yourself down
Do not let your anger show

Alone

To be alone is frightening
And makes you feel afraid
When you have someone else
You seem to have it made

To be alone is spooky
And that no doubt
When alone in darkness
All you want is out

To be alone is awful
And can mess with your mind
You always seem to feel someone
Coming up from behind

To be alone is a challenge
That we all go through
Although you are not really alone
For God is always with you

When You Dis' Me

When you dis' me
You miss me
When you recognize I'm different
And realize I can't see

You so busy looking
You not feeling me

Just because I'm blind
You assume I live in the dark
You'll never know the flame I am
Cause you don't notice my spark

Like a reader skimming only
The cover of a book
You'll never know my story
Without a real in-depth look

Seeing only what I can't
Instead of what I can do
You're missing out on things
That I may have to offer you

So when you dis' me
You miss me
Adding DIS to my ability
You're selling me short
I might be a writer, own a business,
Or even play a sport

But if you can't see past my so-called disability
Then you'll never find
I am funny, creative and intelligent

Not just some person who is blind

So when you see a person with a so-called disability
Be careful what you do
For the reality of the matter is
They are a person just like you

And let me leave you with this thought
Remember auntie Burris said
Sometimes one's so-called disability
Lies only in another person's head

So when you dis' me
You miss me
And you don't know who I am
All you know is that I'm female
Because I answer to ma'am

Made in the USA
Columbia, SC
06 August 2024